On the PLANE
Activity Book

Heather Alexander

Illustrated by Putri Febriana

THIS BOOK BELONGS TO:

_____

_____

IVY KIDS

·CONTENTS·

WORLD
TRAVELER
PASSPORT

When you travel to a different country, you must carry a passport. A passport looks like a little book. It lets people leave and re-enter their country.

Some countries stamp your passport when you arrive. Look at the stamps on this page and draw your own here.

PASSPORT

LAST NAME: - - - - - - - - - - - - - - - -

FIRST NAME: - - - - - - - - - - - - - - - -

NATIONALITY: - - - - - - - - - - - - - - - -

DATE OF BIRTH: - - - - - - - - - - - - - - - -

PLACE OF BIRTH: - - - - - - - - - - - - - - - -

SIGNATURE: - - - - - - - - - - - - - - - -

Your passport includes a picture of you. There are rules for passport photos: no hats, no sunglasses, and no smiling. Draw your own passport picture and fill in your details in the spaces above.

My Boarding Pass

It's time to fly!

To get on an airplane, you need a boarding pass. Fill out the blank boarding pass below. If you don't have a real one to copy, you can just pretend! Make up an airline name and a destination.

Airline Name: _____

Passenger Name: _____

From: _____

To: _____ **Seat Number:** _____

Flight Number: _____ **Date:** _____

Time of Flight: _____

A Look Outside and Inside

Airplanes are ingenious inventions that make the most of the space they have. Let's take a look at the inside and outside of an airplane. Keep your eyes open for FIVE LITTLE MICE and ONE PUPPY that are hiding.
Can you find them?

The **tail fin** keeps the plane flying straight.

Exit doors can be opened in an emergency.

The **cargo area** is where luggage is stored. Some planes also deliver mail, food, furniture, computers, and toys.

Wings help lift the plane into the air.

The **runway** is a long, flat strip of land where planes take off and land.

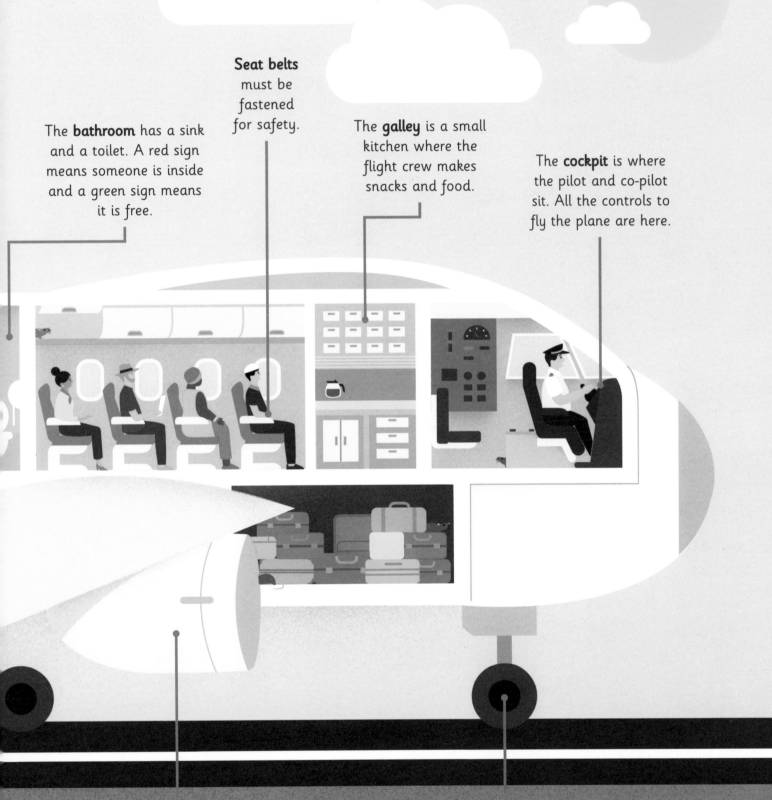

The **bathroom** has a sink and a toilet. A red sign means someone is inside and a green sign means it is free.

Seat belts must be fastened for safety.

The **galley** is a small kitchen where the flight crew makes snacks and food.

The **cockpit** is where the pilot and co-pilot sit. All the controls to fly the plane are here.

Jet engines burn fuel and draw in air to make the plane lift and fly. Most big airplanes have two or four engines.

Landing gear is used for takeoff and landing. Wheels are folded into the belly of a plane after takeoff and lowered for landing.

Runway Ready

Connect the dots to reveal what is waiting on the runway. When you've finished, you can color it in.

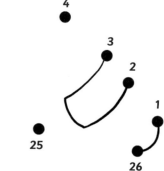

15 ●   14 ●

13 ●

16 ●

12 ●

9 ●

10 ●   8 ●

17 ●

11 ●

7 ●

6 ●

5 ●

18 ●

4 ●

3 ●

23 ●

19 ●

2 ●

24 ●

1 ●

20 ●

22 ●

25 ●

21 ●

26 ●

SYMBOL SUDOKU

People in the airport travel from many different countries and speak many different languages. Airport signs use symbols like the ones below instead of words, so everyone can understand them.

Complete this symbol sudoku puzzle. Fill each square with one of the symbols. Make sure no symbol is repeated—each one can appear only once in each row, column, and mini-grid. Each symbol has a number, so you can write these numbers instead of drawing the symbols if you prefer.

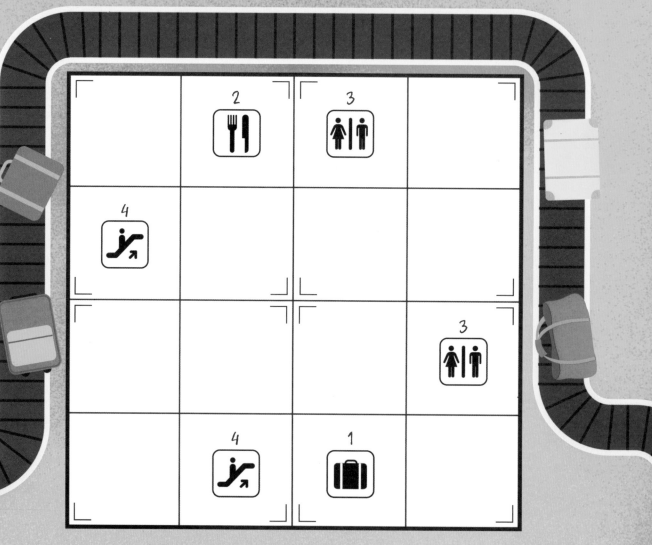

The Waiting Game

The passengers are waiting at a gate inside the airport until it's time to get on their airplane. Can you find and circle:

a pretzel
a bow tie
a dog

the number 76
a flower
a skateboard

High-Flying Design

You've been hired! A brand-new airline wants you to design its airplanes and uniforms. Let your creativity soar!

What will you name the airline?

Choose three colors for your airline (color in the boxes):

Draw a symbol for your airline. You can use an animal, an emoji, a plant, or create your own design:

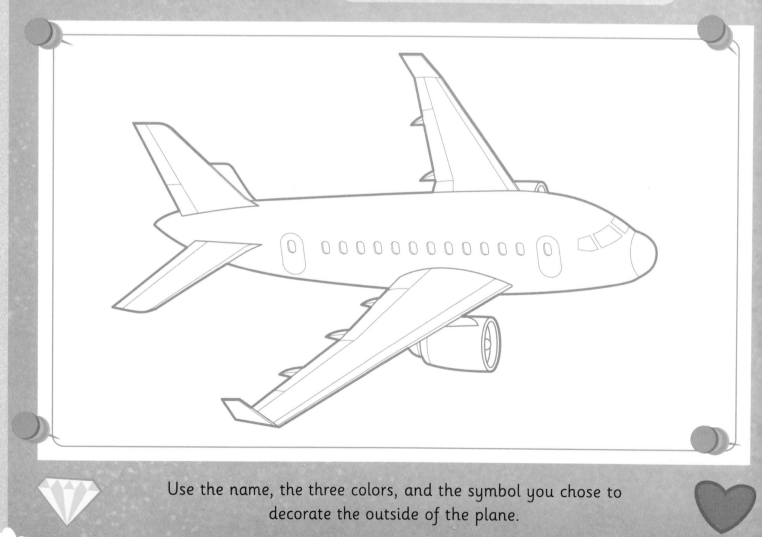

Use the name, the three colors, and the symbol you chose to decorate the outside of the plane.

Now finish designing the uniforms. Add colors, details, and some fun patterns (stripes, polka dots, zig-zags) to the clothes below.

WHAT'S INSIDE?

X-ray machines let security agents see inside luggage without opening it. Let's see what they see. Look at the X-rays of these four pieces of luggage and then read the luggage labels describing the passengers. Can you match the luggage to the right passenger? There are more labels than suitcases so make sure you read them all and match the right ones!

A man traveling with his dog to compete in a dog show.

2

1

A music teacher on her way to her students' concert.

A ballerina traveling home after a performance.

WEIGHT LIMIT

Most airlines have luggage weight limits. Luggage must be under a certain weight or passengers may have to pay extra money.

Use your math skills to help the passengers avoid any extra fees. Each cart of suitcases below should only weigh 10 units in total. Cross out one bag from each cart so that the other three bags add up to 10.

SHADOW MATCH

Many other objects fly, besides airplanes. Draw a line between the high-flier and its shadow. Then write the name of each one on the dotted lines.

- - - - - - - - - - - -

- - - - - - - - - - - -

- - - - - - - - - - - -

- - - - - - - - - - - -

- - - - - - - - - - - -

DESIGN A TRAVEL POSTER

Travel posters hang in the airport to advertise exciting places to visit.

There's one poster space that's empty. Create a travel poster for your hometown or a place you've recently visited. Write the name of the town and draw a picture of something fun to do there or an interesting location to visit.

Busy Runway!

Runways can be busy places. It's important that all planes are in the right places at the right times to avoid any accidents or delays. Each airplane below has a number. Follow the dotted line connected to it to the right runway. Write that number on the runway. The first one has been done for you.

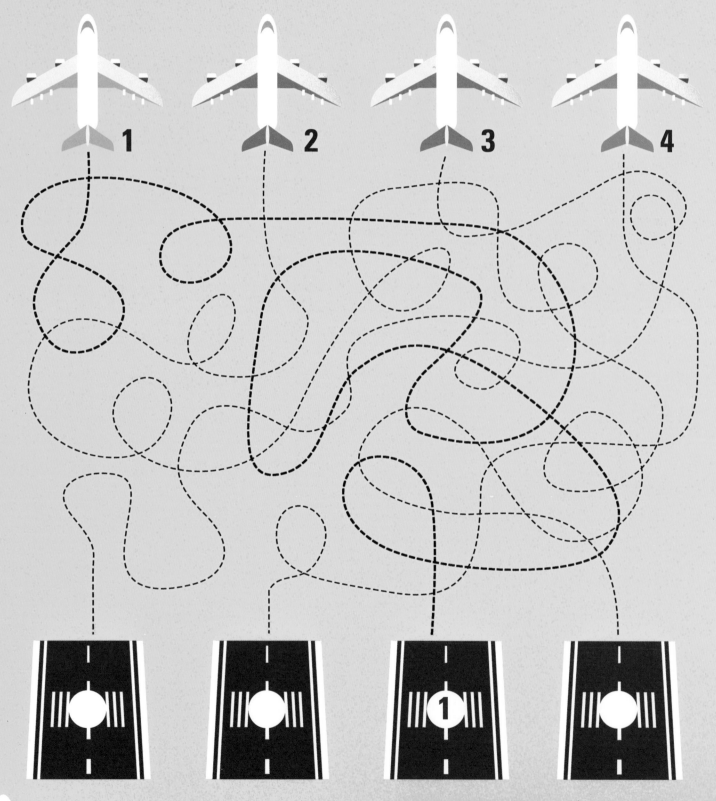

READY TO FLY

Airports are full of people, including captains getting ready to fly their planes. Can you find and circle the two identical captains in the airport below?

Fill-in-the-Face

Airplanes are filled with people of all ages, sizes, and shapes.

Draw the faces of some people who are on your plane or create people on a pretend plane.

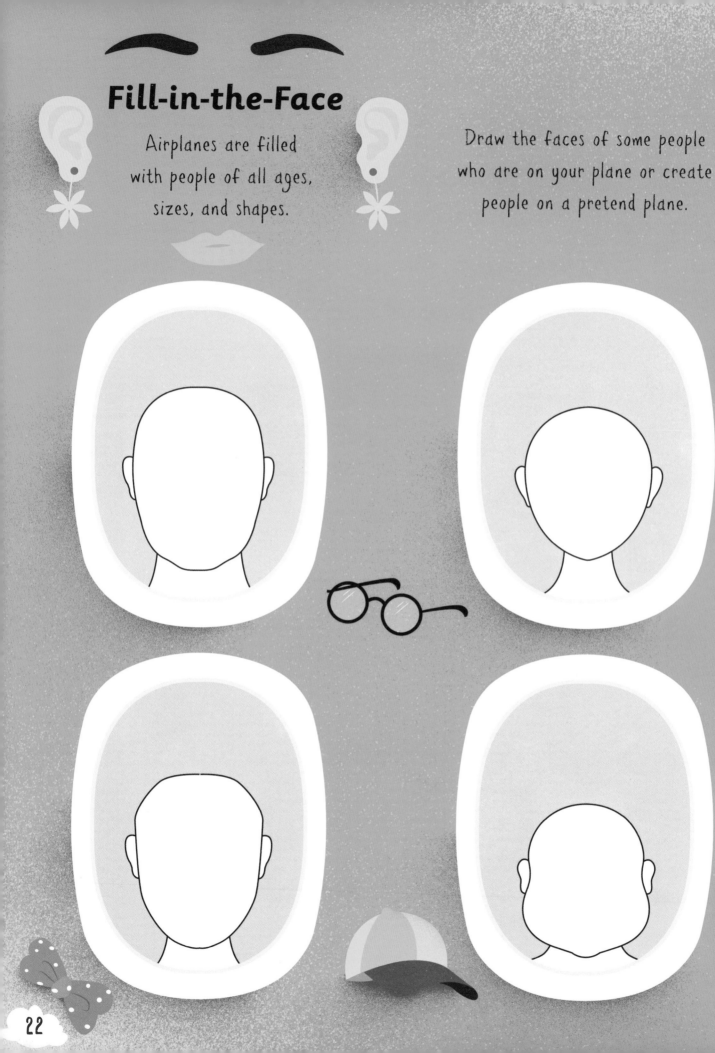

Be creative—add hair, hats, mustaches, freckles, glasses, headphones, jewelry, and eye masks!

What's Different in the cockpit?

The controls to fly a plane are found in the cockpit. The many dials, switches, and lights measure how high the plane is, how fast it's flying, and other important things. Take a look at the two pictures. There are eight differences between them. Can you find and circle them all?

NUMBER JUMBLE

The number codes on the cockpit monitors are all mixed up! Help the captain find them in the grid below. The number codes may be forward, backward, up, down, or diagonal. Some numbers may overlap. Circle or highlight the codes as you find them in the grid.

5	0	6	3	7	5	7	6
2	1	7	8	3	5	8	5
8	8	8	7	6	7	3	8
8	9	3	8	6	3	5	6
9	7	0	2	6	0	7	6
5	4	2	7	1	5	9	6
1	3	1	4	7	9	2	7
2	4	2	4	4	8	6	4

NUMBER CODES:

123	9753	5573
245	9882	84424
866	1479	68815

GUESS WHO?

One of these passengers is a famous movie star! Use the clues below to work out who it is.

Clue 1: They are not eating ice cream

Clue 2: They are wearing something on their head

Clue 3: They are wearing something blue

Clue 4: They do not have a mustache

Clue 5: They have glasses

Clue 6: They have something in their lap

Cross out the passengers as you eliminate them from your search, then circle the movie star once you work out who they are.

WHO WORKS AT THE AIRPORT?

Many people work at the airport. Do you know what they all do?
Check the box if you think the statement is **TRUE** or **FALSE**.

1. "Captain" and "first officer" are the correct names for the pilot and the co-pilot.

TRUE ☐   FALSE ☐

2. A captain has six stripes on his/her shirt.

TRUE ☐   FALSE ☐

3. To be a passenger airplane pilot, you must be more than 40 years old, pass a test, and have had at least 1,500 hours of flight time.

TRUE ☐   FALSE ☐

4. Flight attendants take care of the passengers.

TRUE ☐   FALSE ☐

5. Baggage handlers come to your home and pack your suitcases neatly for you.

TRUE ☐   FALSE ☐

6. Security agents look carefully at all passengers and inside all bags to keep the airplane safe.

TRUE ☐   FALSE ☐

7. Ticket agents at the check-in counters draw a smiley face on everyone's tickets.

TRUE ☐ FALSE ☐

8. The ground control crew wave long peacock feathers to direct planes in and out of the gates.

TRUE ☐ FALSE ☐

9. Mechanics fix any broken parts in an airplane.

TRUE ☐ FALSE ☐

10. Custodians decorate the airport and the airplanes with balloons.

TRUE ☐ FALSE ☐

11. Caterers supply the plane with food and drinks.

TRUE ☐ FALSE ☐

12. Air traffic controllers use computers to see where airplanes are in the sky. They talk to the pilots and tell them when to take off, when to land, and where to go.

TRUE ☐ FALSE ☐

How many questions did you answer correctly? Check in the Answers section and then see what kind of flier you are:

11–12 CORRECT: HIGH FLIER

7–10 CORRECT: GLIDER

3–6 CORRECT: READY FOR TAKEOFF

How to Draw an Airplane

Follow these easy directions to draw your own airplanes on the opposite page.

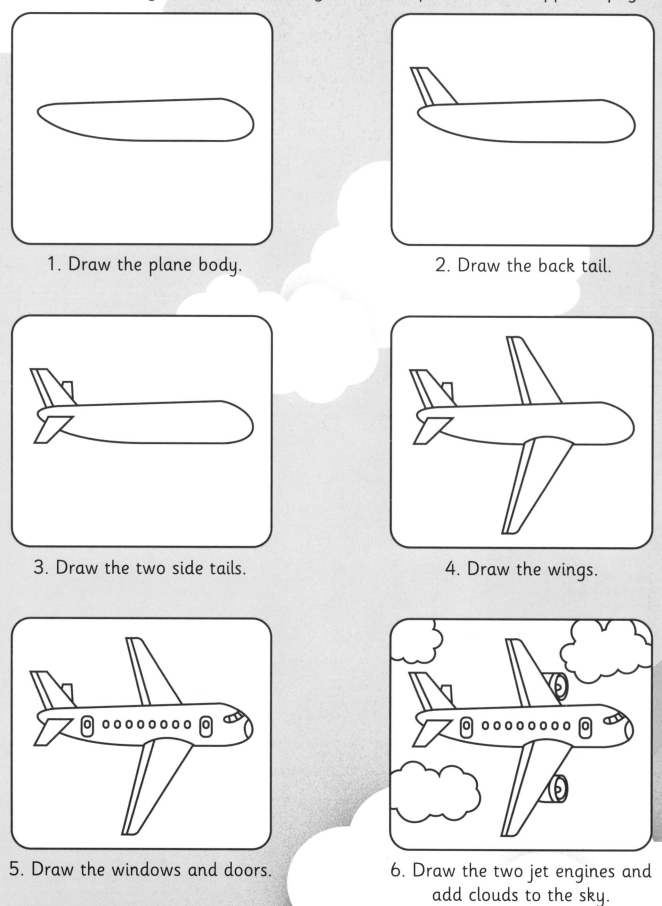

1. Draw the plane body.

2. Draw the back tail.

3. Draw the two side tails.

4. Draw the wings.

5. Draw the windows and doors.

6. Draw the two jet engines and add clouds to the sky.

Fill this page with as many airplanes as you like, then draw some clouds and add in the sun. Finally, color in your picture.

Snack Time

This family brought
five bags of snacks to eat
on the plane. Write down the
snack that's the odd one out in each bag.

1. _ _ _ _ _ _ _ _ _ _ _ _ _ _ _ _ _ _

2. _ _ _ _ _ _ _ _ _ _ _ _ _ _ _ _ _ _

3. _ _ _ _ _ _ _ _ _ _ _ _ _ _ _ _

4. _ _ _ _ _ _ _ _ _ _ _ _ _ _ _ _

5. _ _ _ _ _ _ _ _ _ _ _ _ _ _ _ _

Out the Window

Imagine you're flying in a plane to your dream destination.
Draw it in the window below. Is it a sandy beach? Or a snowy mountain?
Or maybe you're taking a trip into space? Be as creative as you like!

A "No Smoking" sign

A water bottle

Someone with a mustache

A pilot wearing a hat

Headphones

A safety instructions sheet

I Spy
while I Fly
How many of the items or people in this list can you spot on your airplane or in the airport? If you're playing alone, see how fast you can find them all (ask an adult to time you). If you're playing with someone else, see who can find the most.

READY, SET, GO!

A newspaper

Someone snoozing

◀EXIT▶

An exit row sign

A cell phone

A person wearing a shirt with a picture on it

A crayon

Someone eating

A person wearing glasses

An eye mask for sleeping

A black hat

A bathroom sign

A paperback book

A baby

White sneakers

A drinks cart

Someone speaking a language you don't understand

3 closed window shades in a row

34

COUNTRIES & CONTINENTS

The world is BIG! There are so many places to visit. Do you know your countries from your continents? Draw a line to match the countries with their continents. Have you been to any of them?

GERMANY •------- • NORTH AMERICA

• EUROPE

NEW ZEALAND •

• SOUTH AMERICA

KENYA •

• AFRICA

JAPAN •

• ANTARCTICA

CANADA •

• ASIA

BRAZIL •

• AUSTRALIA AND OCEANIA

HINT: One continent doesn't have any countries at all!

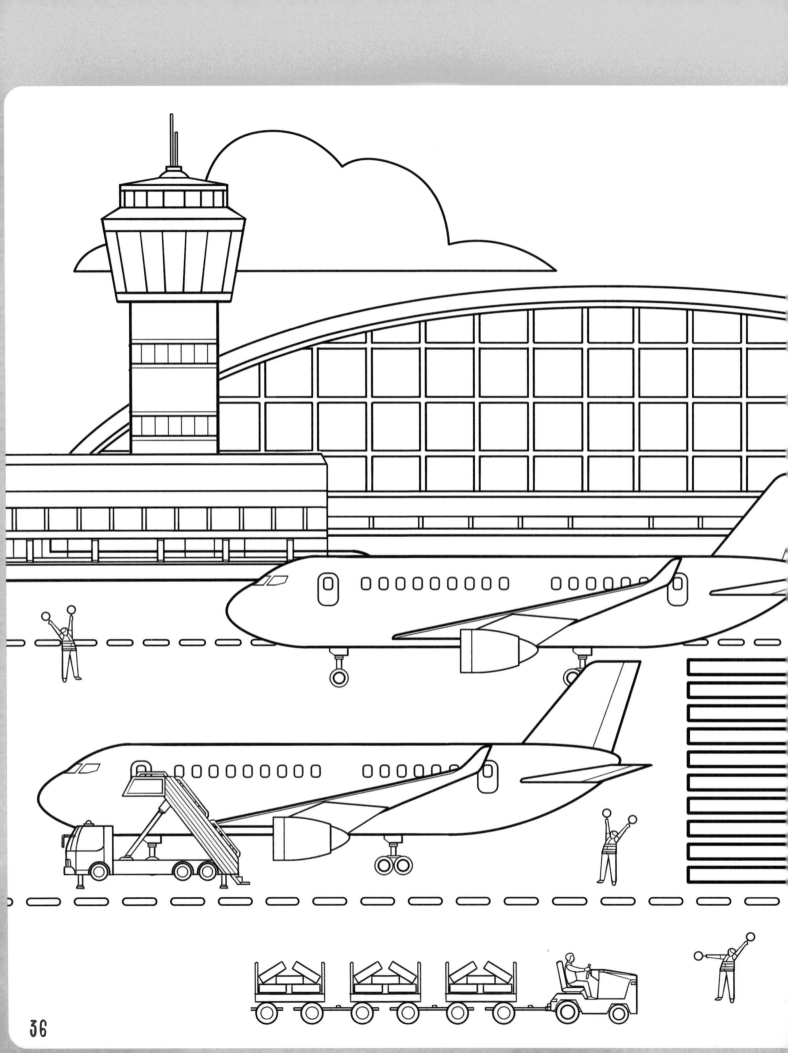

COLORING IN BEHIND THE SCENES

Airports aren't just full of planes—there are many other vehicles,
workers, and buildings that make up these fascinating places.
Color in the busy airport scene below.

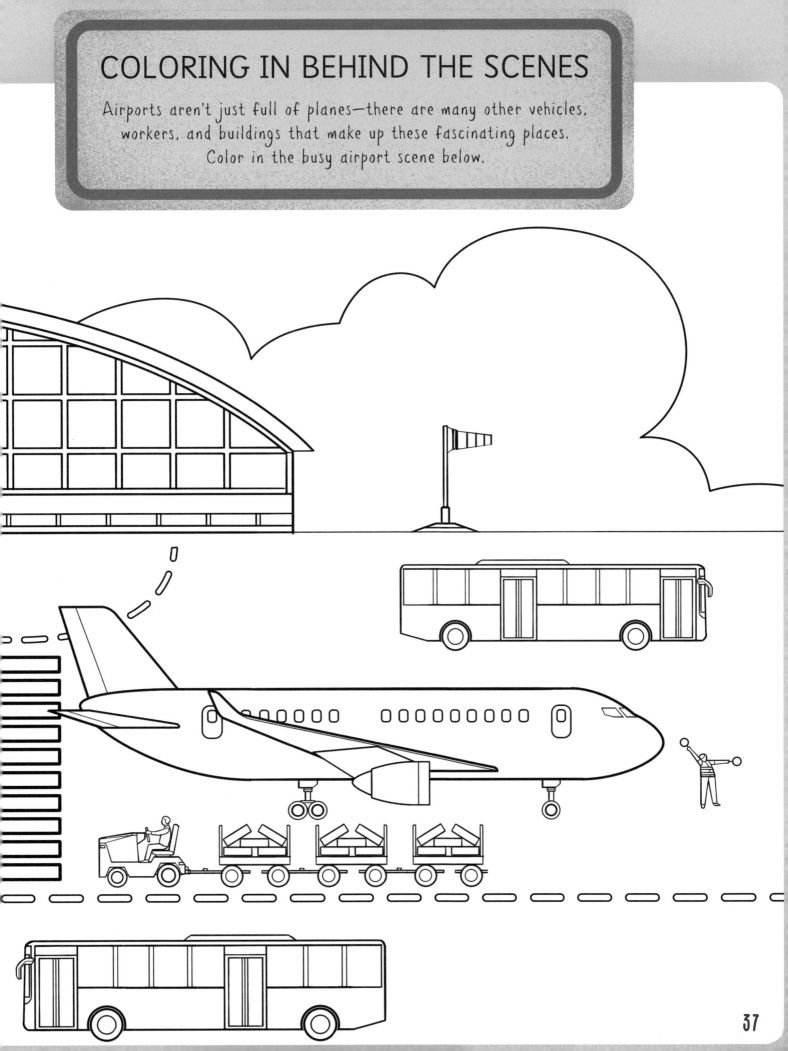

WHO'S FLYING THE PLANE?

There are many different types of airplanes and flying machines. Draw a line to match each aircraft to the right pilot.

Commercial passenger airplanes carry people who have bought tickets from one destination to another.

Bi-planes have two main wings stacked one above the other. Pilots sit with their top halves out of the plane and are exposed to the wind and weather.

Fighter jets are used by special forces for air-to-air combat. They are very fast! Pilots often wear helmets with oxygen masks.

Some helicopters are used as air ambulances to quickly transport people to hospitals in emergencies. Pilots wear fluorescent clothing and have to stay very calm under the pressure.

COUNT THE CUBES

High altitudes make people thirsty, so flight attendants serve drinks on the airplane. Some of the ice cubes in these cups have melted. Circle the cup that had the most ice cubes to begin with.

- 2 ice cubes have melted in cup 1
- 3 ice cubes have melted in cup 2
- 5 ice cubes have melted in cup 6
- 1 ice cube has melted in cup 8

IN THE CLOUDS

Have you ever spotted a cloud in the sky
that looks like an animal or an object?

Use this space to draw the things you
see in the clouds around you.

You could try drawing some cloud fish, a cloud cat, or a cloud car!

ODD ONE OUT

It's not just planes that can fly. Many objects, animals, and machines can fly too.
In each row, circle the one flying thing that is different from the rest.

KNOW THE RULES

There are certain rules that passengers have to follow when traveling on airplanes. Take a look at the rules below and identify the real rules from the false ones. Circle the real ones. One has been done for you.

1a Babies are not allowed on planes.

1b Babies are allowed on planes if they are with an adult.

2a Smoking onboard is forbidden at all times.

2b Smoking is forbidden when the plane is flying.

3a Scissors are never allowed in the cabin.

3b Scissors are allowed in the cabin, if you're a hairdresser.

4a Party poppers are allowed in the cabin on Christmas Day.

4b Party poppers are never allowed in the cabin.

5a Pets must have passports when flying.

5b Only human passengers need passports when flying.

6a Seat belts must be fastened for the whole flight.

6b Seat belts can sometimes be unbuckled during a flight.

7a Assistance dogs are allowed in the cabin.

7b Assistance dogs are never allowed in the cabin.

DOTS AND DASHES

Modern airplanes have the latest radio and GPS technology but in the past it was much harder for pilots to communicate with each other and crews on the ground. At one time, people used radio waves to send messages in Morse Code.

When Morse Code is written, letters and numbers are represented by a series of dots and dashes. Look at the table to see the dots and dashes that represent each letter, then crack the codes opposite.

A	•–	J	•–––	S	•••
B	–•••	K	–•–	T	–
C	–•–•	L	•–••	U	••–
D	–••	M	––	V	•••–
E	•	N	–•	W	•––
F	••–•	O	–––	X	–••–
G	––•	P	•––•	Y	–•––
H	••••	Q	––•–	Z	––••
I	••	R	•–•		

Each code represents the name of a capital city. There is a forward slash between each letter. One code has already been cracked for you.

•– –•• / •– / •–• / •• / •••

P A R I S

1 •_ _/•_/•••/••••/••/_•/_ _•/_/_ _ _/_•   _••/_•_•

ANSWER: _ _ _ _ _ _ _ _ _ _   _ _

2 •_••/_ _ _/_•/_••/_ _ _/_•

ANSWER: _ _ _ _ _ _

3 •_•/_ _ _/_ _/•

ANSWER: _ _ _ _

4 _•••/•/••/•_ _ _/••/_•/_ _•

ANSWER: _ _ _ _ _ _ _

5 ••••/•_/•••_/•_/_•/•_

ANSWER: _ _ _ _ _ _

6 _•/•/•_ _/   _••/•/•_••/••••/••

ANSWER: _ _ _ _ _ _ _ _

7 •_••/••_/_•_/•/_ _/_•••/_ _ _/••_/•_•/_ _•

ANSWER: _ _ _ _ _ _ _ _ _ _

8 Now translate the following letters into Morse Code: SOS

ANSWER: /   /

45

POSTCARD FROM THE PLANE

Write a postcard to a friend, your class, or a family member.
Tell them about a plane journey. It can be real or imaginary.
Then draw a picture on the front of the card.

SHOW OFF YOUR PILOTING SKILLS

Can you fly the plane through the cloudy skies to reach the airport?
Watch out for lightning strikes, flocks of birds, and other obstructions!

WHAT'S FOR DINNER?

MEMORY TEST
The flight attendant brings you a tray of food.
Look at it for one minute then cover the page
and try to answer the questions opposite.

1. What color is the napkin?

----

2. How many pieces of broccoli are on the tray?

----

3. Is the bread plain or does it have seeds on it?

----

4. How many meatballs are on top of the spaghetti?

----

5. Is the cookie chocolate or vanilla?

----

6. What drink is in the glass?

----

7. Which three fruits are in the fruit bowl?

Finish the Silly Letter

This game can be played with as many people as you like. Ask your friends and family to say a word that fits the description below each blank space, or think one up yourself, then write in that word.

The sillier the words, the funnier the letter will be!

No one should know what the letter says until you have all the words needed.

When the blanks are filled, read the letter out loud.

Dear _____,
(Name of friend)

You won't believe who sat next to me on the airplane! _____!
(Famous male person)

We were both going to _____.
(Name of city)

He brought his pet _____. Its name was _____
(Type of animal)   (Girl's name)

and it had _____ eyes. He let her sit in my lap.
(Color)

He told the flight attendant he didn't want food. Instead, he opened his bag and

pulled out a _____.
(Kitchen appliance)

He cooked _____ and _____ .
(Vegetable)   (Dessert)

Then he pulled out a toothbrush and brushed his pet's _____ .
(Body part)

Next, he began to sing _____ in _____ .
(Favorite song)   (Foreign language)

Then he stood in the aisle and did _____ .
(Type of dance)

I began to dance, too. Soon everyone on the plane joined in, even the woman with

the _____ hair and the man with the picture of a
(Color)

_____ on his shirt.
(Type of animal)

We had a dance party until the captain told us to fasten our

_____ .
(Type of clothing)

What a funny plane ride!

Your friend,

_____
(Your name)

Hidden Picture

Color in all the numbered shapes using the key.
How many captain's hats can you find? Write the number below.

KEY

1
2
3
4
5
6
7

O F F   T H E   G R I D

It's very foggy and the captain can't see the airport. Use the directions below to work out where it is so she can land the plane safely. Once you have worked out where a landmark is, draw or mark it on the map, then move on to the next one.

	A	B	C	D	E	F	G	H	I	J
10										
9										
8										
7										
6										
5										
4										
3										
2										
1										

1. The park is in square G2.

2. The school is 5 squares up from the park.

3. The post office is 2 squares right and 2 squares up from the school.

4. The river starts 1 square up and 4 squares left from the post office and also runs through squares: D9, E8, D7, E6, D5, D4, C3, C2, C1.

5. The bridge is 4 squares left of the park.

6. The bakery is 2 squares left and 3 squares up from the bridge.

7. The hospital is 2 squares right and 4 squares up from the bakery.

8. The airport is 2 squares down from the hospital.

Which square is the airport in? _

DESTINATION GAME

These five pieces of luggage have got mixed up at the airport. Use the clues inside the luggage and the destination descriptions below to match up each passenger with their luggage and their destination. Match them up by drawing lines between them. One has been done for you.

Florida, in the US, is one of the most popular vacation destinations in the world. The sunshine, beaches, and amusement parks attract people from all over.

The Umba River in Russia is one of the best places in the world for salmon fishing. Each May people travel to the riverside to try to catch the biggest salmon on Earth—but they sometimes have to compete with bears!

3

The Australian Open is a tennis tournament held every January in Melbourne, Australia. Thousands of athletes and spectators attend from around the world.

4

France is famous for its ski resorts. Professional skiers and snowboarders as well as people on vacation travel to France to whizz down its snowy slopes.

5

The largest international dog show in the world, Crufts, is held every year in the UK. People from all over the world bring their dogs to compete for prizes.

FLIGHT PATH

There are many different routes, or "flight paths," that airplanes can take when traveling from one destination to another. Some journeys last days, with multiple stops along the way for the plane to refuel, and other flights take under 15 minutes!

By moving from plane to plane, can you draw the shortest route from the UK to Norway? You can only use even-numbered planes, and you can't go backward.

74

69

60

39

11

12

75

15

28

79

4

55

56

27

3

20

1

66

9

43

8

35

5

2

30

6

54

14

47

64

59

7

76

31

58

UNITED KINGDOM

NORWAY

50 46 4 72 80 68 17 29 73 25 19 42 13 65 24 51 78 71 10 16 45 22 61 38 63 41 34 62 40 23 32 57 52 18 21 49 77 33 36 67 53 26 37 70 48

Remember: You can go straight,
side-to-side, or diagonally.

57

MY DAY OF TRAVEL

**Fill in this keepsake of your trip.
It can be real or imaginary.**

DATE: _

When I woke up I was in _.

To get to the airport, I took a _.

I traveled with _.

Before we boarded the plane, I _.

The plane ride was _ hours.

The food was _.

I did / did not take a nap on the plane.

↑

Circle your choice.

The plane landed in _____ .

The weather was _____ .

When we arrived at our destination I _____

_____ .

Before I went to sleep I planned three things to do while
we were there:

1. _____

2. _____

3. _____

My next trip will be by:

train / hot-air balloon / bus / boat

Circle your choice.

ANSWERS

PAGES 6–7:
A LOOK OUTSIDE AND INSIDE

PAGE 8: RUNWAY READY

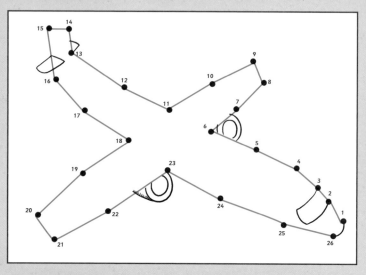

PAGE 9: LAST CALL FOR BOARDING

PAGE 10: SYMBOL SUDOKU

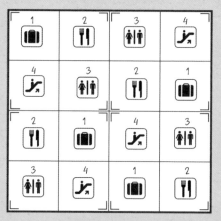

PAGE 11: THE WAITING GAME

PAGES 14–15: WHAT'S INSIDE?

1. A doctor on her way to a conference.
2. A famous chef traveling to film a cooking show.
3. A little boy going on vacation with his family.
4. A ballerina traveling home after a performance.

PAGE 16: WEIGHT LIMIT

PAGE 17: SHADOW MATCH

Helicopter

Rocket

Drone

Hot-air balloon

Kite

PAGE 20: BUSY RUNWAY!

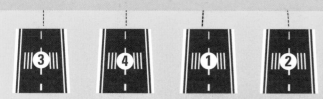

PAGE 21: READY TO FLY

PAGE 24:
WHAT'S DIFFERENT IN THE COCKPIT?

PAGE 25: NUMBER JUMBLE

5	0	6	3	7	5	7	6
2	1	7	8	3	5	8	5
8	8	8	7	6	7	3	8
8	9	3	8	6	3	5	6
9	7	0	2	6	0	7	6
5	4	2	7	1	5	9	6
1	3	1	4	7	9	2	7
2	4	2	4	4	8	6	4

PAGES 26–27: GUESS WHO?

PAGES 28–29:
WHO WORKS AT THE AIRPORT?

1. True
2. False—a captain has four stripes on his/her shirt, two on each shoulder.
3. False—you must be 21 years old or over, pass a test and have had at least 1,500 hours of flight time.
4. True
5. False—you must pack your own bags.
6. True
7. False
8. False
9. True
10. False
11. True
12. True

PAGE 32: SNACK TIME

1. Carrot (the others are fruit)
2. Pretzel (the others are cookies)
3. Cheese (the others are nuts)
4. Donut (the others are sushi)
5. Pineapple (the others are vegetables)

PAGE 35: COUNTRIES AND CONTINENTS

Germany: Europe
New Zealand: Australia and Oceania
Kenya: Africa
Japan: Asia
Canada: North America
Brazil: South America
Odd one out: Antarctica

PAGES 38–39:
WHO'S FLYING THE PLANE?

PAGE 40: COUNT THE CUBES

PAGE 42: ODD ONE OUT

PAGE 43: KNOW THE RULES

Real rules: 1b; 2a; 3a; 4b; 5a; 6b; 7a

PAGES 44–45: DOTS AND DASHES

1. Washington D.C.; 2. London; 3. Rome;
4. Beijing; 5. Havana; 6. New Delhi;
7. Luxembourg; 8. . . . / _ _ _ / . . .

OPEN THIS PAGE FOR
REMOVABLE POSTER
MAP
OF THE
WORLD

MY TRAVEL MAP

Take a look at this map of the world. Which places have you visited and which would you love to explore? Start planning your next adventure!

NORTH AMERICA has heaps to offer, from huge cities like New York, to deserts, beaches, and mountains, as well as animals like polar bears and bald eagles.

In **SOUTH AMERICA** you can trek over the Andes mountains, explore the Amazon rain forest, or visit the awesome Christ the Redeemer statue in Rio de Janeiro, Brazil.

AFRICA is a vast continent. Visitors can go on safari to spot animals like lions, elephants, and giraffes in the wild.

In **EUROPE** there are lots of famous historical landmarks like the Eiffel Tower in Paris, France and the Colosseum in Rome, Italy.

ASIA is the biggest continent in the world and there is plenty to do and see. You can walk along the Great Wall of China or explore the magnificent Taj Mahal mausoleum in India.

AUSTRALIA & OCEANIA is full of incredible creatures, from kangaroos to kiwi birds. But watch out for big scary sharks!

ANTARCTICA is the only continent with no countries. But people still visit. Some even brave the harsh conditions and trek to the South Pole.

OPEN THIS PAGE FOR
REMOVABLE POSTER
MAP
of the
WORLD